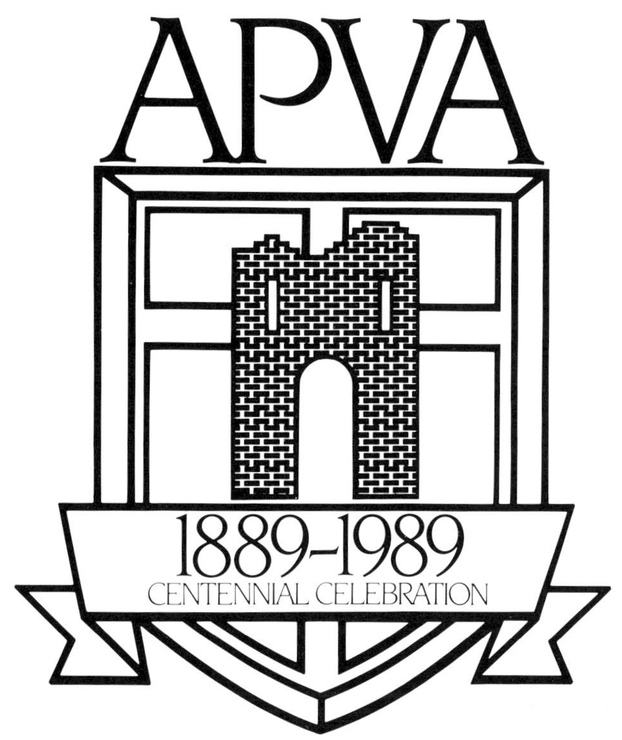
APVA
1889–1989
CENTENNIAL CELEBRATION

White Gloves & Red Bricks

APVA 1889-1989

By Nancy Elizabeth Packer
Curator of Collections

Foreword

What is a centennial? A centennial is a perfect occasion to look back and evaluate an organization over the passage of time, to review its evolution, to determine if it has lived up to the expectations of its founders, to examine its strengths, and to chart its future. The fact that somehow an organization has survived for a century is not sufficient reason for celebration. One needs to be able to say that, despite the inevitable interorganizational tensions and the inconsistencies of human nature, it has kept its eye on what is "proper," and, perhaps more appropriately, that as the "proper" way has changed from one generation to another for over one hundred years, the organization was able to adapt and to adjust its methods in an ever-changing world.

The Association for the Preservation of Virginia Antiquities has chosen to begin the celebration of its centennial year with the presentation of an exhibit, "White Gloves and Red Bricks," to open on the hundredth anniversary of its founding. The centennial exhibit tells a story of the first century of the association from the perspective of the exhibit's curator, Nancy Packer. It is a very positive, insightful story. It shows that we have followed our mandate in the "proper" way.

In planning for the centennial celebration year, the APVA Board of Trustees, related committees, and staff considered many alternatives as fitting means to recognize and give emphasis to the association's distinguished past. An exhibit was found to be a particularly appropriate way to begin the celebration because it could assemble, in one room, the most treasured objects that tell our story. Integral to the significance of the APVA is the fact that, from the very beginning, it viewed its mission as one to preserve and protect Virginia's past on a statewide basis. Today the sizeable collection of properties and objects spans the state from Blacksburg to Virginia Beach and from Leesburg to Accomac. By assembling some two hundred objects, images, and architectural fragments in the exhibit area of our longtime sister organization, the Virginia Historical Society, we can accomplish what is otherwise impossible—to offer an opportunity for an individual to view and reflect upon the totality of this decentralized and complex institution.

The exhibit and its accompanying catalog are certainly not the only scholarly views occasioned by the centennial year. It will be a year of discovery and discussion. Feature articles will appear in *The Virginia Magazine of History and Biography, Virginia Cavalcade, Colonial Williamsburg,* and *William and Mary Alumni News,* and, along with special editions of APVA publications, a centennial series of branch histories will be published. Articles in regional and national magazines and newspapers will spread the word far beyond the borders of the state in which the APVA, Virginia's "historic" historic preservation organization, began.

The APVA has always been much more than the tangible resources represented by the "Red Bricks" in the exhibit's title. APVA people have been a truly remarkable collection as well. During this year we will pay homage to those who have devoted themselves to the APVA cause in the past and join hands with those in the present at numerous happy and proud occasions. A special highlight will be the Centennial Meeting Weekend in May, centered in the Jamestown area, where our nation was born and where the spark for the organization of the APVA was generated.

Please join me in congratulating all of the people in the past and present—the founders, the advisors, the headquarters and branch boards, the staff, and the many members and friends of the APVA—for giving us this uniquely wonderful organization. It has accomplished much in its first hundred years and, with continued help and devotion, it will go on to do much more to preserve the "ancient monuments" commemorating the history of Virginia. We have done so much more than just survive one hundred years. Happy Birthday, APVA.

Bruce MacDougal
Executive Director

January 8, 1989
Richmond, Virginia

Introduction

The Association for the Preservation of Virginia Antiquities (APVA), chartered on February 13, 1889, is America's oldest statewide historic preservation organization. Yet the APVA's value lies not in its preeminence or in its age but in its unique contribution over the past century to American history, through its remarkable success in preserving a broad cross-section of one region's cultural heritage. The present exhibition, "White Gloves and Red Bricks," is a celebration of this success and an optimistic look forward to a second century of accomplishment.

Despite the APVA's diversity in its collections, its activities, and its membership—a diversity which has increased rather than diminished over the passage of a century—a common thread has united APVA people and efforts in the one hundred years of its existence: a dedication to the preservation of Virginia's history for future generations. It was the founders of the APVA, women of established antecedents and prominence in Virginia society, who first recognized this mission and who took upon themselves the burden to pursue their goal against all odds. In the past one hundred years, our methods have changed considerably—in the assessment of historical value, the technical means of preservation, and the communication of information —but the motivation behind these activities has remained constant. It is the intent of this exhibition to trace the course of this preservation impulse over the past century as embodied in the APVA and to commemorate the success which this association has realized in the preservation and presentation of some of Virginia and America's most historically significant sites, structures, and artifacts.

Many individuals and institutions have helped to make this project possible. Our highest debt of gratitude goes to the board and staff of the Virginia Historical Society who graciously made available the Society's exhibit area in Battle Abbey for the installation of "White Gloves and Red Bricks" between February 13 and June 1, 1989, and to the Virginia Museum of Fine Arts for hosting the opening reception on February 13. The catalogue and exhibit were made possible through the generous financial support of the William Byrd Branch of the APVA, Mrs. Ellice MacDonald, Mr. and Mrs. Coleman Donaldson, William Byrd Press, a division of Cadmus Communications, and the numerous donors to the APVA Centennial War Chest. The exhibit opening has been generously underwritten by The Robert W. and Florence S. Cabaniss Foundation and supported by Mr. and Mrs. S. Douglas Fleet. For assistance in research and the securing of photographs and objects for use in the exhibition and catalogue, special thanks are due to Jim Garrett and Ron Hurst, Colonial Williamsburg Foundation; Margaret Cook, Earl Gregg Swem Library, College of William and Mary; Rudy Favretti, A.S.L.A., and The Garden Club of Virginia; Bly Straub, James River Institute for Archaeology, Inc.; David Riggs, National Park Service, Jamestown; Lacy Dick and Colleen Callahan, Valentine Museum; and Herbert G. Fischer, Virginia Division of Historic Landmarks. Outstanding contributions to the catalogue have been made by Tom Chambers, designer; Claire Newman, page make-up artist; Emily and John Salmon, editors; and Katherine Wetzel, who produced outstanding original and copy photographs. Appreciation is also due to Mrs. Catesby G. Jones and Dr. Edward D. C. Campbell, Jr. for reading the manuscript. The talents of Pat Chester, of Chester Design Associates, Inc., exhibit designer, and the advice and assistance of Jeff Nagel, assistant curator of the Virginia Historical Society, have been invaluable. My personal thanks are due for the support of the APVA Celebrations Committee and its chairman, Barbara Donaldson, and for the assistance of the APVA staff. I would like to particularly recognize the unceasing support, enthusiasm, and assistance of Sarah Driggs and Henrietta Lipscomb.

Nancy E. Packer
Curator of Collections

The Preservation Impulse

In 1889, the year in which the Association for the Preservation of Virginia Antiquities was organized, the preservation impulse in America was still a relatively new and nebulous concept. At its root lay a variety of motives (some of which had first become manifest centuries before) but not until the second half of the nineteenth century did these impulses develop and merge into a full-fledged and recognizable historic preservation movement.

The urge to preserve the artifacts of past cultures as objects of curiosity, veneration, and emulation was already discernible in medieval and Renaissance Europe, with the enshrining of religious relics, the collecting of exotic natural curiosities, and the assembling of private art collections. This proclivity for collecting the tangible relics of the past flourished especially in the eighteenth century, particularly with the midcentury discoveries of Roman Herculaneum and Pompeii and the resulting dissemination of classical arts and design through published engravings and design books. A taste for the fashions of the more recent past also emerged in this period, in the replication of elements of the "Gothick" style in furniture, architecture, and landscape. In such monuments to the "Antient" and "Gothick" fashions as the "ruins" of England's highly designed, picturesque landscape gardens of the eighteenth century, the passion for the past began to acquire some of the cultural associations and values that would inspire the emergence of the historic preservation movement in the following century.

The attribution of specific social values and characteristics, such as courage, purity, or patriotism, to the styles, monuments, and artifacts of the past intensified markedly in the Victorian period, as virtually all elements of the concrete world were imbued with new cultural significance and meaning. With the increased communication and more rapid diffusion of information fostered by the nineteenth-century flowering of industrialization, moreover, an even broader range of cultural models became available upon which to draw for inspiration.

At the same time that mechanization provided the means to discover and emulate the past, however, the world's industrialized nations, particularly England and the United

Residence and Tomb of Washington, Mount Vernon.

States, were beginning to experience disillusionment with the more negative aspects of the industrialization process and nostalgia for the perceived virtues of the preindustrialized world. In America, this yearning for the more virtuous pleasures of the past expressed itself most notably through the glorification of the country's revolutionary history, which was interpreted as a moral rejection of monarchical decadence for the virtues of republican Rome. As the figurehead of this righteous rebellion, George Washington had emerged during his own lifetime as a hero of truly monumental proportions to all Americans. It is far from surprising, then, that America's first successful preservation efforts in the mid-nineteenth century were directed toward two structures noted for their association with Washington—the general's revolutionary headquarters in Newburgh, New York, and his home and final resting place along the Potomac River in Virginia, Mount Vernon. The chartering of the Mount Vernon Ladies' Association of the Union in 1856, with the sole mission of preserving Mount Vernon in perpetuity and restoring it as a shrine to the icon of the Republic, was a particularly vivid demonstration of the maturation of the preservation impulse and of the role of women as the perceived moral leaders in this endeavor.

During the antebellum period American women had few opportunities for employment outside the home. Restricted by custom and social pressure to a role of nurturing and protecting family morals, women found outlets for their organizational skills in church and charitable work. The Civil War presented women with new opportunities, particularly in nursing and in civilian relief work, and after the war southern women took the lead in commemorating their dead heroes. Given women's role as nurturers, protectors, and keepers of the flame, it is not surprising that women became leaders in historic preservation as well. Women who were so inclined

found in the preservation movement a socially acceptable means of protecting America's historical values and memorializing the heroes who embodied those values by preserving their artifacts, their homes, and other significant sites.

The highly visible example of Mount Vernon's preservation was a spur to like preservation efforts, as well as an important harbinger of the colonial revival movement in America. It later provided an initial organizational model for the APVA, but its immediate impact on Virginia and the South was lessened by the outbreak of the Civil War, which redirected American funds, energies, and passions away from the nascent preservation movement. By the 1880s, the South was tentatively emerging from the devastation wrought on the economy and spirit of the Confederate states by the war more than two decades earlier. Yet the war's destruction was almost certainly a crucial element in the rebirth of the preservation impulse represented by the APVA's founding. In seeking to negate the images of strife, destruction, and decay stamped on Virginia's countryside by the Civil War and to reestablish the state's pride and preeminence in American history, Virginians turned to the monuments of the state's former glory as the first permanent English settlement in America and as the birthplace and resting place of the leaders of the Revolution and early Republic.

By the mid-1880s, then, a complex range of cultural currents and motivations had merged into the definable goal of the restoration of Virginia's dignity and traditional values through the preservation of her antiquities. Thus compelled, two Virginia women, Cynthia Beverley Tucker Coleman and Mary Jeffery Galt, would independently embark upon the preservation work that ultimately led them to create the first statewide preservation organization in America and one of the earliest associations of its kind devoted to historic preservation—the APVA.

The Founding Years

As early as 1884, Cynthia Beverley Tucker Coleman, of Williamsburg, had turned her energies toward the rescue of Virginia's colonial capital city from the neglect and decay that had descended upon the town since the removal of the capital from Williamsburg to Richmond a century before. Faced by a dearth of funds and a daunting degree of deterioration throughout the old town, Cynthia Coleman gathered together the only resource available to her—the young friends of her recently deceased twelve-year-old daughter, Catherine—and created the Catherine Memorial Society. The society memorialized not only Catherine Coleman but also those values and virtues, such as piety and purity, that were believed to be disappearing along with the tangible monuments of Virginia's past.

With the stated objective of rescuing the Bruton Parish churchyard from the weeds and neglect that threatened its historic tombs, the Catherine Memorial Society by 1886 was actually undertaking the far more substantial mission of restoring the traditional ethics and social code entombed with Virginia's early heroes. In a plea for funds published in the *Southern Churchman* in 1887, Cynthia Coleman wrote that "all of the monuments in the church yard are more or less defaced by time. To restore them, as far as may be, to their original strength and beauty, the children of the Catherine Memorial Society are lending all their energies. They have sold ivy leaves and early spring flowers in New York; have held festivals and made fancy work at home." The preservation achievements of the Catherine Memorial Society ultimately encompassed the repair of several of the historic tombstones in the Bruton Parish churchyard, the reconstruction of the church wall, and the donation of substantial funds toward a new roof for the one-hundred-seventy-year-old church structure.

Even as Cynthia Coleman was marshaling local support for the preservation of Williamsburg's fast-disappearing historic sites, Mary Jeffery Galt, of Norfolk, was alerted to the urgent need to secure the future of Virginia's other colonial monuments. As Miss Galt later wrote of the conception of the APVA:

> *One evening in the early part of June, 1888, my mother came into my room with the Southern*

Opposite page, top: Cynthia Beverley Tucker Coleman, co-founder of the APVA and founder of the Catherine Memorial Society, was responsible for early preservation efforts in Williamsburg.

Opposite page, bottom: Mary Jeffery Galt, of Norfolk, was co-founder of the APVA and played a crucial role in the preservation of Jamestown.

Bruton Parish Church, Williamsburg, as it appeared before its 1903-1907 restoration .

Churchman in her hand. She pointed to a column, on the front page, saying, with tears in her eyes: " The Powhatan Chimney has been blown down, all of our Virginia landmarks are passing away; nothing is being done to save them, before long all will be gone." Then I began to ask myself if something could not be done to save them. Couldn't an association be formed for that purpose?

By the following day, Miss Galt had met with Barton Myers, mayor of Norfolk, to discuss the formation of such an organization, and, at the suggestion of her sister, Annie Galt, and Mayor Myers, had chosen the name of the Association for the Preservation of Virginia Antiquities.

Clearly conceiving of the proposed association as having a statewide, even regional, scope from the very start, Mary Galt sought support for the formation of the organization not only in Virginia, in Williamsburg and Richmond, but also among the numerous expatriate Virginians residing in Washington, D.C., and New York. During a meeting to garner support for her preservation society in Williamsburg, it became apparent that Miss Galt and Mrs. Coleman were working towards the same goal, and the two women joined forces. This meeting culminated in the organization of the Association for the Preservation of Virginia Antiquities at the Tayloe House, Cynthia Coleman's home in Williamsburg, on January 4, 1889.

Receiving its first official charter of incorporation from the commonwealth of Virginia on February 13, 1889, the APVA had a clearly defined mission: "to restore and preserve the ancient historic buildings and tombs in the State of Virginia, and acquire by purchase or gift the sites of such buildings and tombs with a view to their perpetuation and preservation."

Top:
Powhatan's Chimney, Gloucester County, engraving of an early drawing. This old chimney, which legend incorrectly associated with the famous Indian chief, collapsed in a storm in 1888.

Bottom:
The Tayloe House in Williamsburg, site of the first organizational meeting of the APVA on January 4, 1889, and home of Cynthia Tucker Coleman.

The ruinous condition of the Jamestown church tower in the late nineteenth century inspired the zeal of Mary Jeffery Galt and the APVA.

"Cradle of the Nation," by Fred O. Seibel, <u>Richmond Times-Dispatch</u>, May 13, 1927. Several of Seibel's well- known cartoons featured APVA activities and issues.

The "Cradle of the Republic"

From the beginning,...one site above all others has commanded the common interest and devotion of the members of the A.P.V.A. This is Jamestown, whose history continues to challenge the scholar largely because preservation of the site has made it a source of continuing information.

Lester J. Cappon, Director
Institute of Early American
History & Culture, 1967

By July 1889, Mary Jeffery Galt and the Norfolk Branch of the APVA had already identified the preservation goal that became the focal point of the APVA's efforts and visibility for much of the next century—the site of the first permanent English settlement in America, at Jamestown, Virginia.

Jamestown had been Virginia's first center of legislative and economic life, as capital of the colony between 1607 and 1699. With the relocation of the capital to Williamsburg at the end of the seventeenth century, however, Jamestown rapidly dwindled in size and importance, as Williamsburg was itself to do a century later. By the early nineteenth century, little survived of Jamestown's once thriving community but the remains of the mid-seventeenth-century brick tower of the fourth church, "mantled, to its very summit, with ivy." By 1857, deterioration, vandalism, and erosion had taken yet a greater toll, and one visitor to the two-hundred-fiftieth anniversary celebration of the 1607 landing noted that "all that remains at Jamestown is a portion of the tower and walls of the old church and a brick magazine now used as a barn. The graves are very much mutilated—less indeed by the lapse of time than by the ruthless curiosity of man." It is ironic that the spirit of relic collecting that had helped to spur the preservation movement which would ultimately be Jamestown's salvation should also have been instrumental in its initial deterioration.

Almost immediately after it was formed in 1889, the APVA made its first effort to rescue Jamestown from total decay when the Norfolk Branch began negotiations to buy the church ruins and surrounding land. Because the organization could not raise

Chinese chair and stand were exhibited at the 1907 Exposition.

"Isobel Lamont Stewart Bryan," by William Garl Brown, oil on canvas, 1889. Belle Bryan, president of the APVA from 1890-1910, and her husband, Joseph Bryan, were key figures in the acquisition and early development of Jamestown.

enough money to purchase even a small portion of the site, it asked the state legislature for title to the state's holdings, which the APVA received in 1892. The following year, Mr. and Mrs. Edward Barney, the new owners of the rest of the land, donated the church ruin and twenty-two and a half acres to the APVA. From 1893 on, Jamestown became for the APVA "this sacred charge…at once our inspiration and our goal."

The attitude of members of the association towards Jamestown for nearly half a century was peculiarly reverent in tone, due only in small part to the religious nature of the ruins themselves. As early as 1895, a tradition was initiated of celebrating the May 1607 settlement of Jamestown through a ritualistic "pilgrimage" to the site, first by steamship and later by automobile, to honor "the shrine of patriotism." In the same spirit, a "Relic House" was built on the site, to display such hallowed artifacts as Pocahontas's birchbark

The Jamestown Exposition site at Hampton Roads, 1907.

basket. A 1907 guidebook to Virginia even likened the site to the great pilgrimage shrines of the world:

> *The Far East has its Mecca, Palestine its Jersualem, France its Lourdes and Italy its Loretto, but America's only shrines are her altars of patriotism—the first and the most potent being Jamestown; Jamestown, the sire of Virginia, and Virginia the mother of this great Republic.*

One vice-president of the APVA was convinced that the preservationists responsible for the salvation of Jamestown would receive their reward in Heaven and would "be found in the Van of the great army of patriots, who shall on some glad 'day of days' plant the triumphant banner of A Risen Sun, upon the ruined walls of Jamestown." Through the employment of such overtly sacred imagery in the service of its secular perpetuation of a particular social

Long-time APVA officer, Mrs. J. Taylor Ellyson was prominent in the APVA's tercentenary celebrations at Jamestown. Her husband was Virginia's lieutenant-governor, as well as a governor of the Jamestown Exposition.

Top:
At the first organized pil-
grimage to Jamestown in
1895, greenery linked the
stage to the desolate site,
while flags and prints elic-
ited historical associations.

Bottom:
The Bryan family donated
the memorial to Captain
John Smith erected in 1909
on the APVA grounds at
Jamestown.

and moral code, the APVA thus legitimized its actions and objectives in a subtle, but characteristic late-nineteenth-century fashion.

Jamestown was also the means by which the APVA would achieve its greatest recognition for its preservation efforts for more than fifty years. Due to its highly visible nature as a national monument, Jamestown attracted attention on a national—and even international scale—beginning with the $10,000 appropriation made by the federal government in 1894 for the construction of a breakwater needed to halt the further destruction of the island through erosion. In the first years of the twentieth century, when the enthusiasm and energy that had founded the APVA showed signs of waning and membership began to diminish, it was Jamestown and the international celebration in 1907 of the tercentenary of its founding, which reinfused the preservation spirit of the association and provided the first supplemental funds for future

Top:
The Memorial Church at Jamestown, shown here under construction, was unveiled by the National Society of Colonial Dames of America on May 11, 1907.

Bottom:
Drawing of details of the obelisk erected at Jamestown by the federal government in 1907.

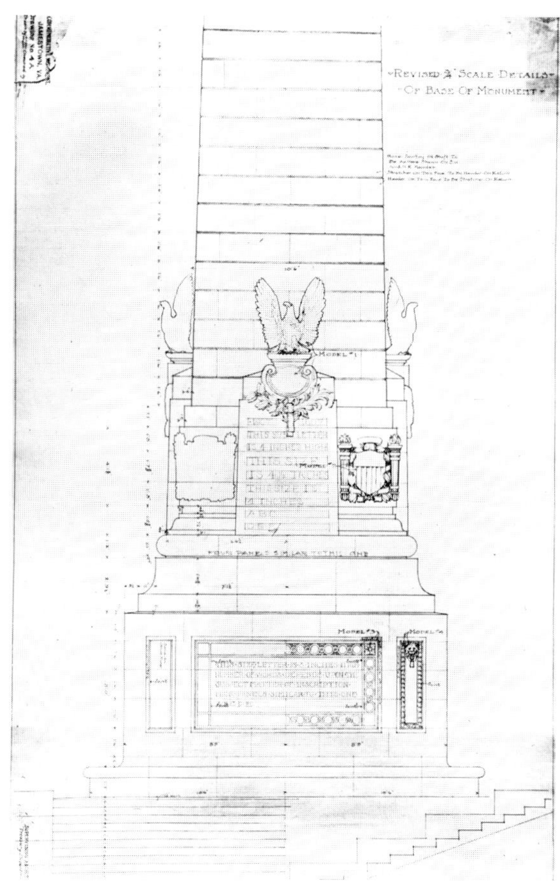

preservation efforts. Though much of the attention during the tercentenary was directed at the yearlong official Jamestown Exposition in Norfolk, where special buildings and exhibits were constructed by the federal and state governments at a cost of several million dollars, the historic site of the settlement received considerable publicity as well, and requests to erect memorials at Jamestown by various groups inspired by the celebration poured in throughout the first decade of the new century. Among the monuments placed at the site during these years by such organizations as the National Society of the Daughters of the American Revolution, the Society of Colonial Wars, and the Protestant Episcopal church, the most notable were the Jamestown Memorial Church funded by the National Society of the Colonial Dames of America, inspired by Saint Luke's Church near Smithfield, and a 103-foot obelisk erected by the United States government at a cost of

$50,000—both of which remain key elements in the modern visitor's perception of Jamestown.

On occasion, such widespread attention was less than welcome to the leaders of the APVA and its Jamestown Committee. One speculator formulated grandiose plans for the island's commercial development in the 1890s, and as early as 1903, there were intimations of the federal government's interest in the site for a national park. A series of resolutions adopted at that time warned that the APVA would vigorously challenge any attempts to wrest from it its "sacred trust for posterity." With the organization of the National Park System in 1916, however, federal involvement, with funds and expertise that the APVA could not hope to match, became increasingly inevitable, and in 1941 the APVA entered into a cooperative agreement with the National Park Service, which settled questions of joint admissions, excavation and research on APVA property, and other matters of concern to both parties. With the existence of a national park at the site, tourism at Jamestown and the site's resulting visibility steadily increased.

A key figure in the administration of Jamestown during these crucial years was Ellen Bagby, daughter of George W. Bagby, the noted southern antebellum author, and Lucy Parke Chamberlayne Bagby, first chair-

man of the Jamestown Committee of the APVA. Ellen Bagby served as chairman of the Jamestown Committee for thirty years, from 1930 until her death, and oversaw virtually all elements of the administration of the APVA's grounds at Jamestown, from gift shop purchases and publicity to archaeological excavations and fund-raising for the maintenance of the seawall. In 1957, when the three-hundred-fiftieth anniversary of the 1607 landing once again focused the international spotlight on the site, and Jamestown hosted more than seven hundred thousand visitors, it was Miss Bagby who escorted Jamestown's most celebrated tourists, Elizabeth II, queen of England, and Prince Philip, duke of Edinburgh, about the APVA grounds.

Ellen Bagby, who was dauntless in her preservation efforts at Jamestown in the face of all adversities, perhaps epitomizes the pioneering preservationist spirit that built the APVA. In May 1960, just two months before her death, Jamestown's "historical archangel" was honored by the Colonial Williamsburg and the Jamestown foundations for her contributions to the preservation and enhancement of the island. In his presentation speech on the occasion, Carlisle Humelsine, then president of the Colonial Williamsburg Foundation, saluted the spirit and achievements of Miss Bagby: "for much of her full life she has been a kind of one-woman task force defending Jamestown from the river, from vandals, from neglect, and from the combined onslaught of the elements and the machinations of man."

Today, the historic grounds of the APVA and the National Park Service at Jamestown attract nearly half a million visitors annually, and the architectural and archaeological development of the site continues to challenge modern scholars of early Virginia—a state of affairs that would undoubtedly gratify the spirits of those valiant early preservationists who fought seemingly overwhelming odds to secure its preservation.

Chairman of the APVA's Jamestown Committee for thirty years, Ellen Bagby was presented with a medal by Carlisle Humelsine, president of the Colonial Williamsburg Foundation, in 1960.

Katherine Wetzel

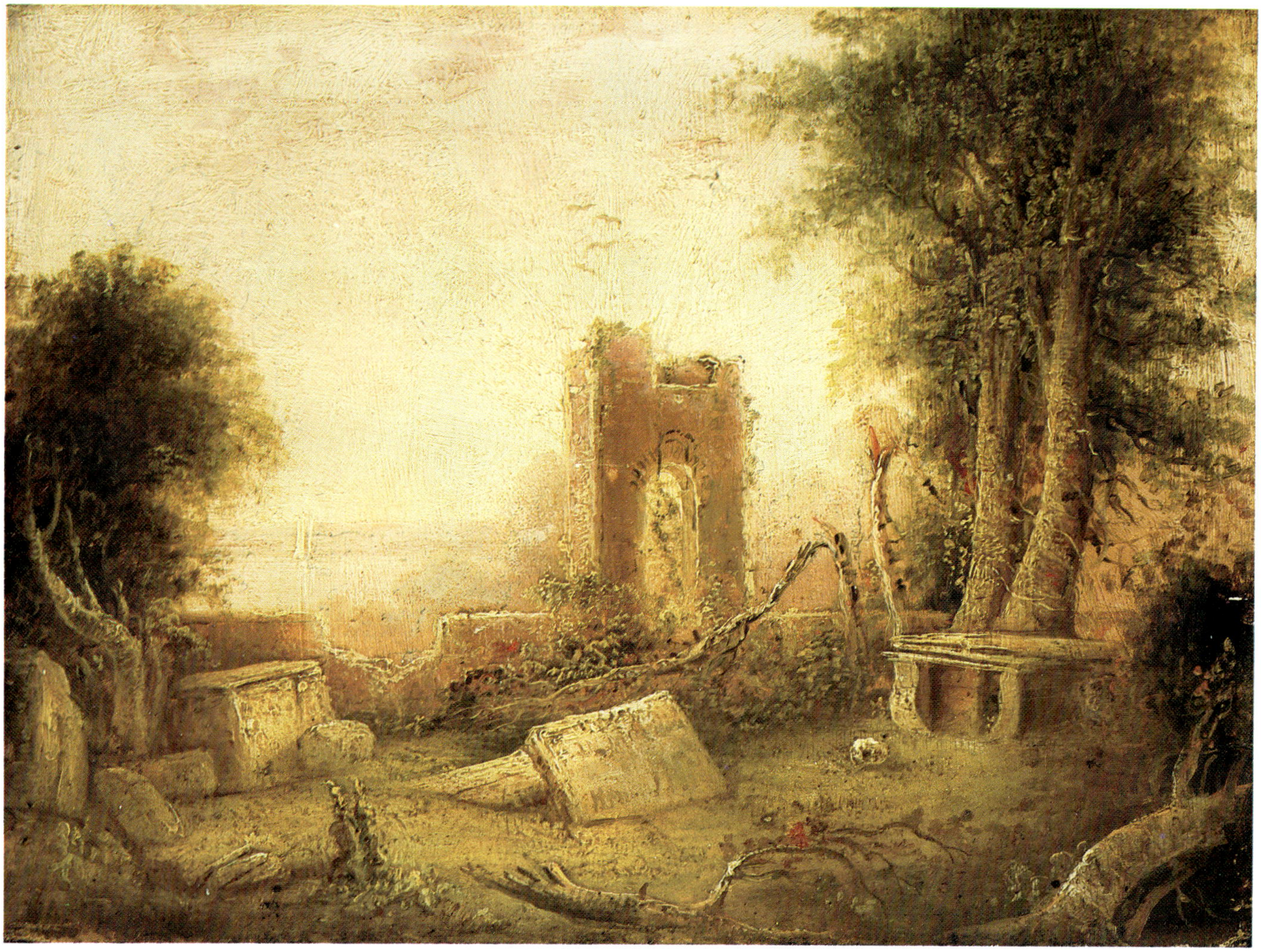

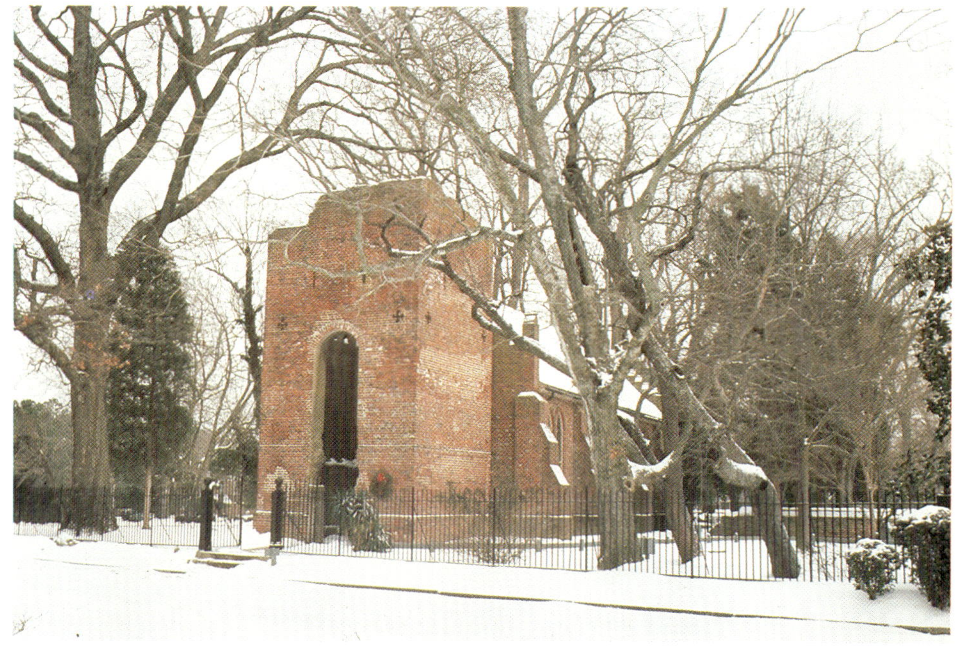

Top:
Ruins of Jamestown Tower, by H. J. Brent, oil on canvas, 1845.

Bottom:
The church tower and Memorial Church at Jamestown, about 1980.

Top:
Smithfield Plantation, built in 1774 on Virginia's western frontier by William Preston, is administered by the APVA's Montgomery County Branch.

Bottom:
The Lynnhaven House in Virginia Beach features late-seventeenth-century characteristics, although research revealed that it was not constructed until 1724.

Top:
Scotchtown, Patrick Henry's home and a National Historic Landmark, is now operated as a historic house museum by the Hanover Branch of the APVA.

Bottom:
A watercolor of Scotchtown, painted about 1800 by J. D. G. Brown, provided architectural evidence for the APVA's restoration of the structure and outbuildings.

The APVA leased the Powder Magazine to Colonial Williamsburg in 1946 and sold it to the foundation in 1986.

"The First Restoration of Williamsburg"

lthough the preservation of Jamestown was the preeminent inspiration and goal of the association from its earliest days, the APVA directed its first successful preservation efforts toward the historic structures of Williamsburg. Of primary concern was the 1714-1716 Powder Horn or Magazine, which had been the site of the 1775 struggle between the colonists and Virginia's royal governor, John Murray, earl of Dunmore, who had ordered the confiscation of the colony's arms and gunpowder and who was later forced to flee from the irate colonists to a British man-of-war in the Yorktown harbor. During the nineteenth century, the Powder Magazine had fallen into an alarming state of disrepair and, by 1880, in use as a horse stable, it was being rapidly encroached upon by new construction on the surrounding green. In 1888, after one wall of the structure had collapsed, Mary Galt identified the Powder Magazine as "the first object to be taken hold of, researched, and repaired" by the projected association, and the preservation of the Powder Magazine became the immediate goal in 1889 of Cynthia Coleman and the Colonial

Capital Branch, the APVA's regional branch organization in Williamsburg. Despite the sometimes difficult negotiations with the owner of the magazine's site, the APVA managed to secure the structure in 1889 for $400 —a seemingly small debt that nevertheless took the infant organization some time to repay. The APVA thus began its century of preservation by assuring the survival of a monument loudly proclaiming Virginia's position as a staunch defender of liberty and democracy in America's early history.

The APVA undertook considerable preservation work in Williamsburg over the next few decades. In addition to the Powder Magazine, which was stabilized and opened to the public in the 1890s as a "Relic House," the APVA acquired by donation in 1897 the Capitol foundations, which were later excavated, protected, and marked with a plaque memorializing the colonial signers of the Non-Importation Agreements. The APVA obtained and marked the remains of the icehouse of the royal Governor's Palace. In 1929, the city of Williamsburg deeded to the APVA the colonial jail building. The association also arranged for the reinterment of several early graves in the

Opposite page, top:
The APVA maintained Williamsburg's colonial jail until its reversion to the Colonial Williamsburg Foundation in 1933 and subsequent restoration.

Opposite page, bottom:
Dr. W. A. R. Goodwin, c. 1897-1901. Goodwin, the rector of Bruton Parish Church and an early APVA member, directed the first restoration of the church in 1903-1907 with the APVA's backing and later spearheaded the Rockefeller restoration of Williamsburg.

Top:
One wall of the deteriorating Powder Magazine (1714-1716) in Williamsburg collapsed before its acquisition by the newly formed APVA in 1889.

Bottom:
The APVA excavated and capped the foundations of the colonial capitol in Williamsburg which it had acquired in 1897, then erected a granite monument on the site.

Bruton Parish churchyard and helped to fund the 1903-1907 restoration of the church under the guidance of Bruton's rector, Dr. W. A. R. Goodwin, a member of the APVA's Colonial Capital Branch. Goodwin later spearheaded the restoration of Colonial Williamsburg with the financial backing of John D. Rockefeller, Jr. The APVA made an effort to place markers on other historic sites and structures in Williamsburg, including the homes of George Wythe and Peyton Randolph, the 1716 theater, and William Parke's printing shop, where the *Virginia Gazette* was first published in 1736.

The efforts of the APVA and its Colonial Capital Branch in Williamsburg were crucial not only to preserve the relics and stave off the effects of decay and age, but also to relieve the considerable pressure on the town of uncontrolled commercial development in the early decades of the twentieth century. In addition to shouldering a debt of $3,000 to preserve the open lot fronting the Powder Magazine, the APVA also twice lobbied the

Williamsburg city council to preserve the city's open greens from modern construction, once successfully in 1901 and then again with less favorable results. The association also resisted the temptation in 1916 to make a substantial profit on its initial investment in the Powder Magazine, when speculation over the proposed construction of a Du Pont munitions plant in Williamsburg led one eager developer to offer the APVA $16,000 for the magazine and the surrounding land.

Throughout its involvement in Williamsburg's preservation, the APVA's primary intention was to promote the best interests of the structures under its care. Thus, as the ambitious scale and aspirations of the Colonial Williamsburg Restoration under Rockefeller's aegis became apparent in the late 1920s and '30s, the APVA began a long period of cooperation with Colonial Williamsburg. The local branch director remarked, "It is a great joy and satisfaction to us to know that so many of the historic landmarks of Williamsburg are to be rescued, preserved and restored. We are giving to this endeavor our cordial endorsement and support." The Colonial Capital Branch's 1930 annual report expressed at greater length the significance of the Rockefeller restoration to the preservation efforts of the APVA:

> *We feel that the Restoration of Colonial Williamsburg is the vindication and fulfillment of the cherished hopes of the founders of our Association. We are further convinced that the emphasis placed by the Association for the Preservation of Virginia Antiquities upon the importance of preserving for posterity the shrines and memorials of Virginia's glorious past contributed in no small measure to create the conviction and to give the inspiration which has led to the Restoration of*

West elevation of Williamsburg's restored colonial capitol, by Perry, Shaw and Hepburn, 1930. The APVA deeded the capitol foundations to the Colonial Williamsburg Restoration in 1928 to facilitate its reconstruction.

Opposite page, top: The colonial jail, after its restoration by Colonial Williamsburg.

Opposite page, bottom: The only surviving late-Victorian structure (c. 1890) in Williamsburg's Historic Area, the Dora Armistead House was leased by the APVA in 1986 from the Armistead family and is now operated as a house museum.

Colonial Williamsburg. The City restored will bear perpetual witness to the vision and to the devotion of the founders of the A.P.V.A. Furthermore, the report continued, "the Colonial Capital branch feels that the sacred purpose of this Association was and should ever be not only to preserve, but also to encourage the preservation of Virginia antiquities. Our pride should be not in the ownership of antiquities, but in the sure guarantee of their continued preservation."

In this spirit, the APVA made an outright gift of the Capitol foundations to the Restoration in 1928, with the stipulation that the Colonial Williamsburg Foundation should restore the building, after review of extensive archaeological and documentary research by a restoration committee including APVA representatives. The remains of the Palace icehouse were likewise donated to the foundation, and, due to the APVA's inability to undertake exten-

sive restoration of the colonial jail, it reverted to the Colonial Williamsburg Foundation in 1933, followed in the same year by the APVA's gift of the two surrounding acres.

The APVA continued to maintain and operate the Powder Magazine in the midst of the Colonial Williamsburg restoration effort, although the offer of Colonial Williamsburg to research and restore the Magazine, "in the light of the best available evidence," was gratefully accepted and carried out between 1934 and 1935. Finally, in 1946, the APVA made the difficult decision to relinquish its responsibility for the first monument under its care, through a long-term lease arrangement with Colonial Williamsburg. In a 1945 letter the director of the Colonial Capital Branch revealed the general sentiment of relief from an overwhelming burden: "We have struggled for so long with the questions of heating and taking care of the Powder Horn under present conditions, and have already met with such generous help and cooperation from Colonial Williamsburg that we are confident the best interests of the APVA would be forwarded by such an arrangement." Furthermore, the lease of the magazine to the foundation freed APVA funds for diversion "to the care and preservation of other Virginia antiquities which are falling to decay with no one to care for them and with no money with which to preserve them."

The same impulse motivated the outright sale of the Powder Magazine to Colonial Williamsburg forty years later. By 1986, however, the APVA had taken on a new custodial role in Williamsburg, through its lease and museum operation of the sole surviving Victorian home within the confines of the Historic Area, the Dora Armistead House. Appropriately enough, the builder of the Armistead House in 1890 was a young Williamsburg lawyer, Cary Peyton Armistead, who, just a year before building his home, had notarized the APVA's founding charter.

*The Mary Washington
House, Fredericksburg,
shortly after its acquisition
by the APVA in 1890.*

"A Branch of the Antiquarian Tree"

Though loosely modeled at first on the Mount Vernon Ladies' Association, the APVA very quickly began to diverge from this example and to assume the organizational form in which it exists today. While its official headquarters was established and continues to be in Richmond, the mere awareness of an endangered monument or historic site in another area of the state was always enough to spur the formation of a branch in that locale to generate sentiment and support for an all-out preservation effort.

Thus, in 1890, just one year after the APVA's founding, Frances Tucker Carmichael, an APVA member residing in Fredericksburg, alerted members of the association to plans then being made "by parties in the North" to purchase the Fredericksburg home of George Washington's mother, Mary Ball Washington, and to dismantle it for exhibition at the Chicago World's Fair of 1893. As the Mary Washington House was perceived to be a particularly potent symbol of the traditional values of early Virginia that the founders of the APVA were seeking to revive, "the whole Association was roused" to thwart this scheme, and the Fredericksburg, or Mary Washington, Branch was founded. Though starting its existence with the considerable debt of $4,000 and a membership numbering as few as nine in the early years of its existence, the branch nevertheless undertook the repair and, later, the restoration and refurnishing of the Mary Washington House. By 1907, still with a membership of just fifteen, the branch had already undertaken the preservation and restoration of the Rising Sun Tavern, the second acquisition of the four eighteenth-century Fredericksburg properties now under its care.

As word of the APVA's preservation endeavors and successes spread in the first decade of its existence, a vast network of branches grew rapidly throughout the commonwealth and beyond. By 1896, thirty-one branches had been formed, including those of New York, Washington, Baltimore, Brooklyn, and Saint Paul, and membership ranged from Chicago to Boston and Minnesota to Texas. Many of these early branches later became inactive and required reorganization or ultimately disbanded, particularly after initial enthusiasm began to wane in the early 1900s.

Katherine Stetson

Similar preservation organizations also began to emerge elsewhere in the country and to vie for local attentions, but the APVA owes much of its past success and present diversity to the efforts of these early branches. As the APVA yearbook for 1934 noted, "it is…plainly evident that these branches…constitute centers of culture for the dissemination of information concerning our early history, and for awakening interest in the preservation of our relics and landmarks." Whether through substantial contributions to the state organization made by affluent out-of-state branches, such as the defunct New York or still vital Nashville

The Rising Sun Tavern in Fredericksburg was rescued from further decay in 1907 by the Mary Washington Branch of the APVA .

Opposite page, bottom: The Mary Washington House in 1988.

Top:
A "working day" held to clean up Warner Hall graveyard by the Gloucester Branch of the APVA, about 1920.

Bottom:
Virginia Tech students visited Smithfield Plantation in Blacksburg shortly after its acquisition by the APVA in 1959 with Dr. George Green Shackelford, director of the Montgomery County Branch.

Top:
Smith's Fort Plantation in Surry County, shown here during a 1938 APVA meeting, has been operated as a historic house museum by the Thomas Rolfe Branch since its donation to the APVA by John D. Rockefeller, Jr. in the 1930s.

Bottom:
The birthplace of Walter Reed in Gloucester County was acquired by the APVA in 1968 and restored by the Joseph Bryan Branch.

branch organizations, the identification and funding of local preservation projects, or the outright acquisition and restoration of historically important local sites, the branch network of the APVA has ensured throughout the past century that crucial preservation goals have been identified and achieved at the local as well as at the state and national levels.

Today, the APVA numbers twenty-three branches throughout Virginia, as well as in Nashville, Tennessee, and Washington, D.C., which are responsible for the maintenance and administration of some twenty-five historic properties and sites around the commonwealth.

Program from the APVA
Kirmess of 1896.

"A Notable Function"

From its earliest days, the APVA has frequently been called upon to raise substantial funds at short notice to purchase and preserve such imminently endangered sites as Jamestown and the Mary Washington House. One of the most successful solutions to this situation in the early years of the organization's existence was through its fancy dress charity balls or "Kirmess." As early as 1890, the association held its first fund-raising ball, billed as a "Colonial Assembly," and began a decade of spectacular presentations that attracted Richmond's highest society and served to heighten considerably the organization's visibility in its home city.

The primary attraction of these events was the carefully staged pageant or "spectacle" that preceded the start of the public dancing. Though intended to be vaguely historical in nature, these performances ranged from "a grand tableau of the Nations and procession led by the Queen of the Kirmess and twenty-four Egyptian attendants" to the lavish production in 1899 of *A Midsummer's Night Dream*, which called upon the talents of Miss Lulu Curtis Vass, "Teacher of Expression and

May Handy, a noted Richmond belle, reigned as Queen of the Kirmess at the 1896 gala.

Top:
"Gordon and Claire
[Smith] as they appeared in
the 'Kirmess' Jan. 1896."
Printed by Homeier and
Clark, Richmond. The
APVA's fancy dress balls
reflected the contemporary
fascination with exotica.

Bottom:
Bryce Hume and Marion
Robins wore Elizabethan
costume to dance the
Sarabande at the 1892
festivities.

Physical Culture," and some forty fairies and dancing sprites.

The last and perhaps most memorable of the APVA's social extravaganzas was held in 1923 and was described in the president's report for that year in vivid detail:

The beautiful Historical Pageant
representing the "Presentation of
Pocahontas at the Court of James
First of England," which was held
at the Grays' Armory on January
27th, far surpassed in brilliancy
and spectacular effect any produc-
tion ever given by the Association.
Princes, Princesses, Ambassadors,
Archbishops, Titled Ladies and
their escorts, the Lord Mayor of
London, Lord Chief Justice, Gen-
tlemen and Ladies of the Court
and others to the number of nearly
one hundred, all resplendent in the
dress of the period, heralded by a

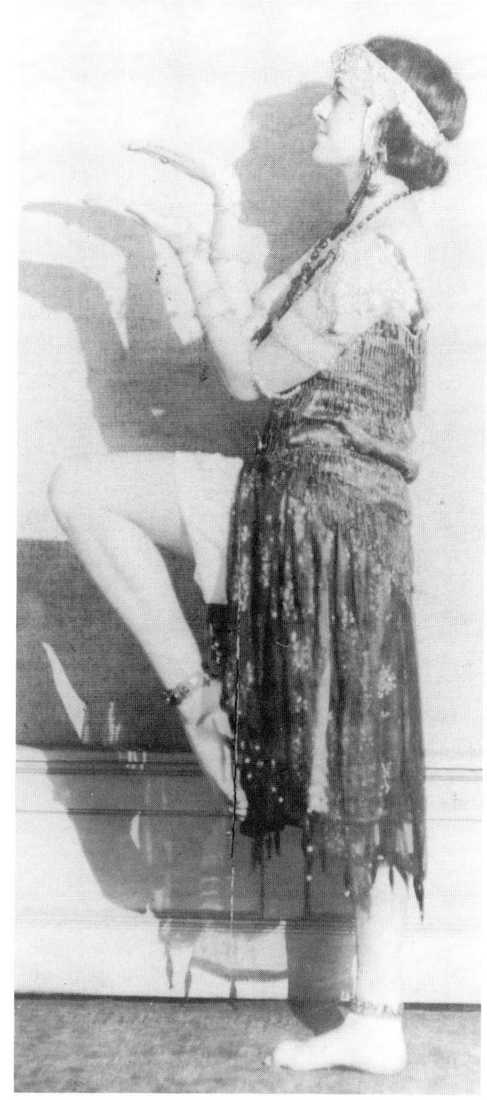

blare of trumpets,were presented to their King and Queen amid a large and enthusiastic assembly of Richmond Society occupying boxes, floor seats and the gallery. Following the Pageant were artistic dances, and before the floor was cleared for the ball, the King and Queen led the Grand March of the Court. It was an evening of rare enjoyment.

Top:
Ernistyne Jean Bachrach performed "a beautiful ancient dance" at the 1923 APVA pageant.

Bottom:
The highlight of the last APVA ball in 1923 was a reenactment of the presentation of Pocahontas to the English court.

A gift from King Charles II to Cockacoeske, the queen of the Pamunkey Indians, this silver badge was the first "relic" purchased by the APVA after its founding in 1889.

Stained glass windows commemorating Nathaniel Bacon and Governor Alexander Spotswood illuminated the Powder Horn Museum. The windows were removed in Colonial Williamsburg's 1934-1935 restoration of the magazine.

A pair of mussel shell earrings set in silver and steel, believed to have belonged to Pocahontas, entered the APVA's collection in 1941.

Great Hall, John Marshall House, 1988. The APVA restored paint colors, plaster moldings, and period wallpaper in the 1970s.

Bacon's Castle, Surry County, watercolor, c. 1820. This image shows the frame wing added in the eighteenth century to the original 1665 brick structure.

Bacon's Castle, Surry County, after restoration by the APVA. The hyphen joining the original structure of 1665 (on the left) and the wing of 1854 (on the right) was constructed in the twentieth century.

Furnishings plans for
"Over the Chamber" in
1711 (above) and the
"Hall" in 1755 (below) at
Bacon's Castle were based
upon detailed period inventories. Watercolor sketches
by Pamela Mather.

The "Hall," at Bacon's Castle, as restored to its 1755 appearance.

Wine bottle discovered during the 1901 excavations at Jamestown.

The New Preservation

he Kirmess tradition was highly evocative of Victorian Americans' nostalgia for the past and the strong social element inherent in the APVA's early activities. Its passing in the early twentieth century was clearly symbolic of the association's changing nature and emergence into the professional world of historic preservation—a world that did not exist in 1889.

Nevertheless, the seeds of professionalism were apparent even in the earliest preservation efforts of the APVA. Mary Jeffery Galt, in particular, was noted for her progressive preservationist sentiment, which dictated extensive research and minimal restoration. She was commemorated by the Alpha Chapter of Phi Beta Kappa at the College of William and Mary in 1922 as "one of a small group of Virginians ardently devoted to historical research...consecrated to the preservation of everything that would aid future generations to understand Virginia history." It was Miss Galt who initiated and supervised the first excavations of the seventeenth-century church foundations at Jamestown in 1897 and again in 1901—an activity that later earned Jamestown

the sobriquet the "birthplace of historical archaeology in the United States" by J. Paul Hudson, for many years museum curator of the National Park Service at Jamestown. The image of Mary Jeffery Galt digging with her own hands in the rubble at Jamestown, as she reported on the excavations in 1897, to uncover the foundations of one of the earliest remnants of English settlement in America is one that vividly reflects the determined spirit that inspired the founders of the APVA.

Jamestown continued to be the focal point for the APVA's professional activities in the early twentieth century, particularly under the direction of Samuel H. Yonge, the engineer who had supervised construction of the federally funded seawall at Jamestown, completed in 1901. Yonge was responsible for virtually all the research, excavation, and restoration activities carried out at Jamestown for three decades, including the extensive 1903-1907 excavations of the APVA grounds, which revealed the foundations of the fourth statehouse and which Yonge documented in *The Site of Old "James Towne,"* first published in 1903. Yonge also supplied the preliminary design for the memorial church erected at

The 1901 excavations, supervised by Mary Jeffery Galt, uncovered the foundations of the third church at Jamestown.

Samuel H. Yonge, supervising engineer of the federally-funded seawall project at Jamestown and author of The Site of Old "James Towne."

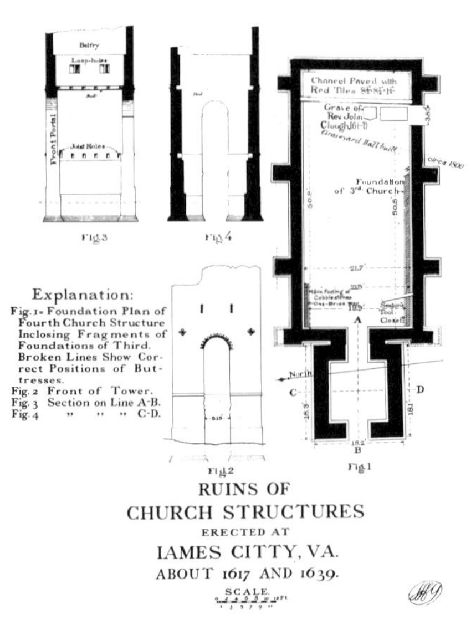

Drawings of the foundations of the third and fourth churches and elevations of the church tower at Jamestown also appeared in Yonge's book.

Jamestown by the Colonial Dames in 1907, basing his design on both the archaeological evidence of the original Jamestown structures and the still extant Saint Luke's Church near Smithfield, of roughly contemporary date. Yonge acted as historical consultant throughout the years for the APVA on numerous projects other than Jamestown and was a key member of the "Committee of Five Gentlemen" responsible for final approval of the restoration plans for Williamsburg's colonial Capitol in the 1930s.

The national and international attention that the activities of the Colonial Williamsburg Foundation and the National Park Service in Virginia earned in the 1930s and 1940s invited a new scrutiny of the preservation efforts of the APVA, even as a new standard of professionalism in historic preservation was being set by these larger and wealthier organizations. With international attention focused on Jamestown during the

Top:
"The Brick Church Restored," by Samuel H. Yonge, ink on paper, 1903. Yonge's rendering for the restored church at Jamestown, based on Saint Luke's Church near Smithfield, illustrated his book The Site of Old "James Towne."

Center:
An APVA membership meeting addressing the issue of "The New Preservation" was held at the Rising Sun Tavern in Fredericksburg in 1969.

Bottom:
Scotchtown, Patrick Henry's home in Hanover County, suffered from neglect for several decades before its purchase by the APVA in 1958.

three-hundred-fiftieth anniversary celebrations in 1957, the APVA found itself in the position of struggling to keep abreast of rather than to create trends in preservation in Virginia. An additional pressure came from the acquisition and maintenance of an increasingly illustrious portfolio of structures, including Scotchtown in Hanover County, Smithfield Plantation in Blacksburg, and Petersburg's Farmers Bank. The challenge that faced the organization was set forth plainly in a 1959 membership solicitation: "Our past has seen fundamental changes all around us and the future must not find us unprepared. By our very success we have created greater demands upon ourselves. We must rededicate and, if necessary, re-educate ourselves."

In this spirit, the APVA employed its first full-time professional executive director in 1968 and began its rapid reemergence into a position of leadership in Virginia preservation. Extensive architectural, archaeological, and

Top:
Rising Sun Tavern in
Fredericksburg before the
APVA reconstructed the
front porch in 1974-1978.

Center:
Porch for the Rising Sun
Tavern, by Walter M.
Maccomber, 1975. One of
the proposals for the recon-
struction project.

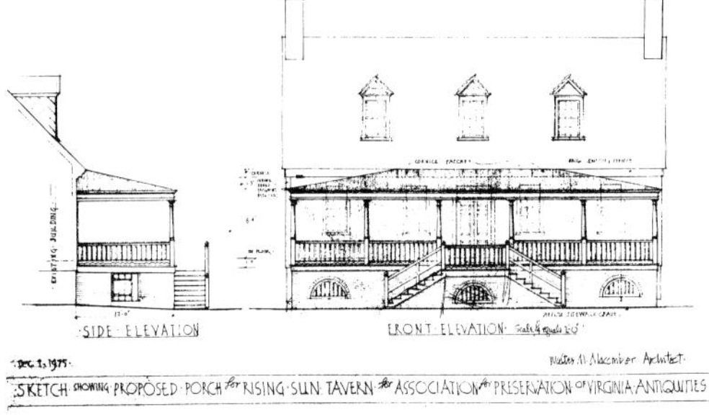

Bottom:
Rising Sun Tavern, after
1978, showing the porch as
rebuilt according to archi-
tectural and archaeological
evidence.

documentary research has characterized the association's restoration efforts since the 1970s, in some cases requiring substantial revisions of earlier restoration efforts. One longtime possession of the APVA—the Rising Sun Tavern in Fredericksburg—took on a surprising new face with the 1974-1978 restoration of its eighteenth-century porch, a feature that had disappeared long before the site came into the APVA's hands in 1907.

Significant new holdings, such as the Lynnhaven House in Virginia Beach, acquired by the APVA in 1971, were also the recipients of and helped to forward the research and restoration technology advances made by the association in these years. Due to its incorporation of such late Jacobean characteristics as a steeply gabled roof, massive end chimneys, exposed chimney joists, and a simple hall-parlor plan, Lynnhaven House had long been regarded as an extraordinarily intact survivor from about 1680. The discovery of a diamond-shaped windowpane under the interior stair of the house during the 1970s' restoration was used as evidence for the replacement of the existing sash windows with leaded casement windows with diamond-shaped panes that were fully in keeping with the other late-seventeenth-century stylistic features of the structure.

Despite such seemingly incontrovertible stylistic evidence of the house's late-seventeenth-century construction, the APVA continued its intensive investigation of the site in the early 1980s, through additional archaeological research and through dendrochronological analysis or tree-ring dating of the original timbers of the house—a process originally developed under the aegis of the APVA in the 1970s in its investigation of Bacon's Castle. By funding a study by the American Institute of Dendrochronology to establish a tree-ring series for the lower Tidewater region to which

the samples taken from the Lynnhaven House could be compared, the APVA discovered that "one of the most completely intact seventeenth century dwellings in English North America" was in fact a remarkable, nearly intact example of seventeenth-century stylistic features still in use in 1724, the year in which the Lynnhaven House was constructed, according to the results of the tree-ring analysis. The archaeological excavations conducted concurrently on the site also substantiated a construction date of about 1725, even as they supported the APVA's earlier decision to restore the leaded casement windows, by unearthing a fragment of turned lead, dated 1730, from such a window. The APVA's investigation and restoration of the Lynnhaven House thus challenged other preservationists and historians of early Virginia culture to reexamine long-held assumptions concerning the endurance and transmission of style in the colonial Tidewater.

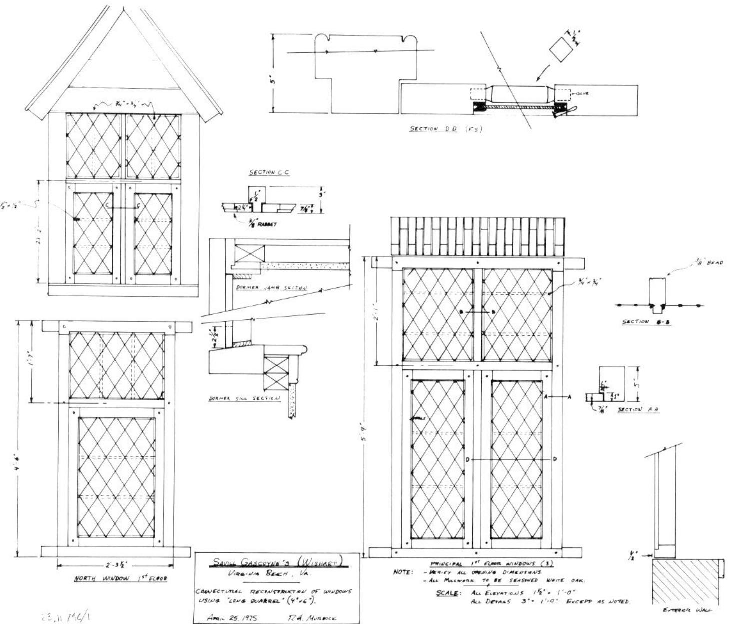

*Interior of the Powder
Horn Museum,
Williamsburg, c. 1900,
where the APVA enshrined
"interesting Colonial relics."*

From Relic Houses to Historic House Museums

From its earliest days, the APVA began to build a collection of objects associated with early Virginia history along with its assemblage of significant Virginia structures. As early as 1890, the association made the first payment towards acquisition of "an Indian crown of silver presented by Charles the Second to the Queen of the Pamunkey Indians," purchased at a cost of $800—twice the sum for which the Powder Magazine had been secured the previous year. By 1892, the APVA's constitution specifically provided that the association was empowered "to receive and protect any relics which may become its property by gift or purchase."

The highly symbolic, even sacred, quality attributed to the objects collected by the APVA in its earliest years was clearly evident in the selective acquisition of objects that were perceived to exert powerful social and moral influences by virtue of their association with such mythic figures as Pocahontas, Powhatan, or Washington. The "Indian Crown" was lauded in this vein as "one of the most beautiful relics of the relation existing between the white man and Indian."

The associational value of these objects was heightened by their enshrinement in displays or "Relic Houses," like those initiated by the APVA at Jamestown and at Williamsburg, in the Powder Horn Museum, where "each article marked by the owners' name is carefully preserved in the interests of the public, and for the honor of the State thus represented." The Powder Horn Museum became the repository of "a few interesting Colonial relics," "the armorial bearings of the early Presidents and Governors of the Colony, beginning with John Smith, and closing with Lord Dunmore," and two stained-glass windows of Governor Alexander Spotswood and Nathaniel Bacon, the latter's window conceived as a "memorial to his patriotism and suffering." Furthermore, the display was envisioned as "a place of public resort and interest." As Cynthia Coleman reminded the APVA's members in 1896, "many northern and western tourists visit Williamsburg as the ancient Capital of the Colony of Virginia. Such

John Marshall House, Richmond, c. 1890. Built by Marshall in 1790, the house was entrusted by the city of Richmond to the APVA in 1911, climaxing a heated preservation battle.

Opposite page, top: View of the southwest room, first floor, John Marshall House, c. 1890. Marshall's descendants still lived in the house at this time. Original possessions of John Marshall appear alongside later family furnishings.

Opposite page, bottom: This photograph of the same room was taken shortly after the house was opened to the public by the APVA in 1913.

a building illustrating that period of Virginia history would be of great value, and redound to the honour of the State."

While the APVA continued as late as the 1930s to collect such reliclike objects as Pocahontas's earrings and birchbark basket, the association also realized that these items must be displayed in a historically accurate context. The APVA's Fredericksburg properties were the first to be treated as historic house museums, as the original portion of the Mary Washington House had been "restored as it was in the days of Mrs. Washington" by 1904, and by 1910, "the quaint interior" of the Rising Sun Tavern had "been made to reflect the setting of an inn in the olden time."

It was not until 1911 when the city of Richmond entrusted the APVA with the administration and maintenance of the John Marshall House, however, that the association consciously undertook the comprehensive and systematic restoration of a site to a specific

historic period. As the yearbook for 1912 reported, "the Association pledged itself to restore and furnish the building as nearly as possible as it was when occupied by its owner." Appealing to Marshall's descendants for the donation or loan of "those things which either belonged to him personally or were the property of any members of his family," the chairman of the John Marshall House Committee reminded members that "the house will be gradually furnished, as it is the intention of the committee to use only those furnishings which were of the design and style used when the house was furnished in 1789." The target date of the restoration was later expanded to reflect the entire period of Marshall's residency, between 1790 and 1835.

With this goal firmly set, the APVA began the restoration of the John Marshall House—a constant process of modification that is ongoing even today. While the Marshall House has been open to visitors since 1913, the changes that have taken place over the past seventy-five years in the interior appearance of the house are an instructive microcosm of the shifts in the concept of historic house museums and furnishings plans in the museum world at large. The John Marshall House Committee, which oversaw the restoration and refurnishing of the property during the APVA's first sixty years of administration, adhered firmly to its fundamental commitment to historical authenticity, particularly in strictly verifying Marshall's association with the numerous objects offered to the house throughout the years. Even so, the development and maturation of the scholarly study of historic interiors, decorative arts, and social history that occurred during this period ensured that the appearance of Marshall's restored home would not remain static.

In the 1970s, with the newly created professional position of curator of collections, the APVA embarked on a new phase of the Marshall House restoration, combining technological and documentary research to re-create as nearly as possible the historic settings for the remarkable collection of original furnishings that had been returned to the house over the years. The primary achievements of this effort were the restoration of original paint colors and architectural finishes, the installation of wallpapers reproduced from original documents of the period, and the fine-tuning of collections, furniture placement, and window treatments based upon Marshall's account books and personal property tax records. Despite the thoroughness of the mid-1970s restoration of the Marshall House, the restoration effort at the house continues today, with the ongoing evolution and refinement of our perceptions of the man, his period, and his possessions.

Bacon's Castle, Surry County, as it appeared about 1890. The Greek Revival wing and porch were added to the east (right) side of the original brick house in 1854.

"Allen's Brick House"

While the historical significance of the Marshall House was relatively simple to isolate and thus interpret to the period of John Marshall's occupancy, the APVA faced a more challenging dilemma of restoration and interpretation with its purchase in 1973 of Bacon's Castle, in Surry County. Bacon's Castle has long been recognized as a highly significant architectural monument, characterized by Virginia's Division of Historic Landmarks as "the state's, if not the nation's, outstanding example of 17th-century domestic architecture," comprising such high-style Jacobean features as offset, clustered chimney stacks, curved gables in the Flemish manner, and a cruciform plan with full-height projecting central bays. Constructed by Arthur Allen I in 1665, as documented by dendrochronology, the unique structure was briefly occupied by the rebel forces of Nathaniel Bacon during Bacon's Rebellion of 1676, from which it derived its name and mythic stature.

Despite its obvious significance to Virginia's seventeenth-century history, Bacon's Castle was continuously occupied for more than three centuries, until the APVA acquired it in 1973. Substantive evidence of these three hundred years was left by the various inhabitants of the property. Modifications to the house over the centuries included the removal of the original seventeenth-century entrance, the construction of a frame wing in the eighteenth century (later removed and relocated nearby), the addition of a massive brick wing and two-story verandah in the Greek Revival style in 1854, and the development of an assemblage of outbuildings, which range in date from the eighteenth to twentieth centuries. The documentary evidence surviving for the dwelling is also remarkable for its scope and span over time, including Arthur Allen II's claim for damages suffered in the rebel occupation of the house in 1676, no fewer than seven detailed inventories of the house's furnishings recorded between 1711 and 1871, and an extensive selection of correspondence and photographs of nineteenth-century vintage.

The APVA and its executive director at the time, R. Angus Murdoch, were thus faced with the challenge of selecting the time period to which Bacon's Castle should be restored and interpreted—the brief interval between the property's construction and its three-month occupation by the rebellious colonists or the three-century span substantially represented in the existing features of the structure and its surroundings. As a comprehensive restoration of the dwelling to its seventeenth-century appearance would have required significant destruction of all evidence of later occupation, including the eighteenth-century interior paneling and fireplaces, the 1854 wing, and most of the farm complex, and would have involved considerable conjecture in the restoration of such features as the original entrance, windows, and porch stair, lacking satisfactory proof of their original appearance, the APVA made the decision to stabilize the structure in its modern state and to interpret the site as it had evolved throughout the centuries.

Having determined that the house would be presented as it would have appeared at different moments in its history, the APVA then established the periods to be depicted and the space in which each would be best interpreted. In the first phase of the restoration of Bacon's Castle, which was completed in 1985, two periods were chosen for interpretation, according to the room-by-room inventories of the dwelling recorded in 1711 and 1755. The 1711 inventory was deemed to be representative of the house's appearance in the seventeenth century, as it had been taken upon the death of Arthur Allen II at age sixty, and it was unlikely that major alterations were made in the last years of his life. Furthermore, the description of items in the 1711 inventory indicated that late-seventeenth-century forms and styles predominated in the furnishings of the house at that time.

In order to place these early forms in the most accurate context, a room in the dwelling, designated in the inventories as "Over the Chamber," which had been altered relatively little through the centuries, was cho-

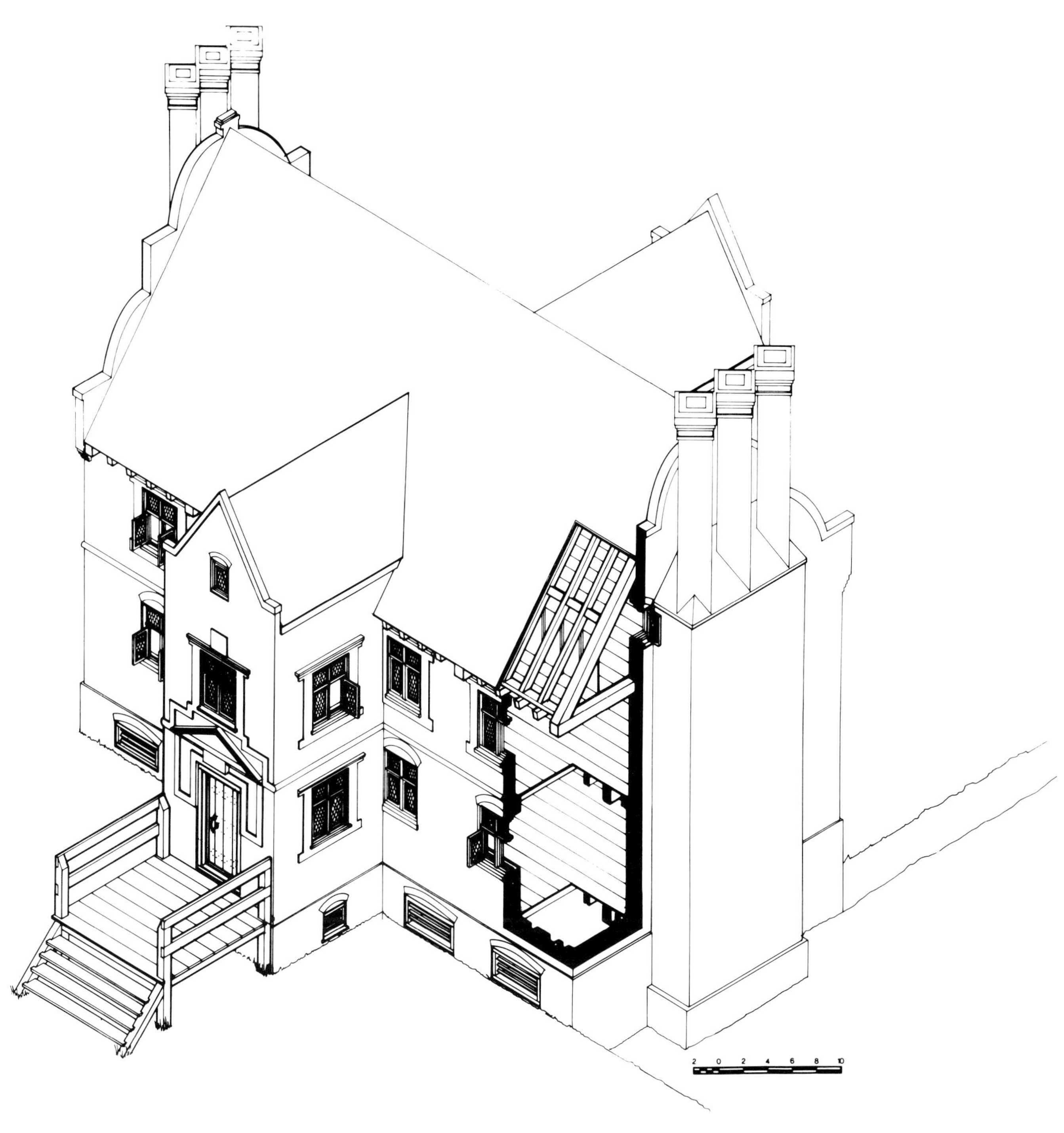

Conjectural isometric drawing of Bacon's Castle as it appeared in 1665, by Stephen A. Smith, ink on paper, 1985.

sen to depict the house in 1711. This decision necessitated the removal of late-nineteenth-century and twentieth-century finishes to reveal the intact massive seventeenth-century fireplace and lintel and exposed ceiling beams. In addition, to simulate the original seventeenth-century fenestration, "false" casement windows with leaded, diamond-shaped panes were fitted inside the window embrasures behind the existing nineteenth-century sash windows.

Interpretation of the house as it appeared in 1755 required fewer modifications, as both of the first-floor rooms of the dwelling's original portion had retained their mid-eighteenth-century raised-panel woodwork throughout the nineteenth and twentieth centuries. The "Hall" was selected for this phase of the restoration, as it would have been the primary formal room of the house from the time of its construction until well into the nineteenth century. It also provided an enlightening lesson in the pace of changing fashions in colonial Virginia, as many of the furnishing items that were present in this room in the 1711 inventory continued to be in use as late as 1755, though supplemented by some newer elements, while others had been relegated to less-public spaces in the house as they fell out of taste or service. By combining such specific information about the furnishings with research into general period interiors and furniture placement, the APVA's curators were able to form a remarkably complete conception of the appearance of Bacon's Castle at two moments in its history and, utilizing both period objects and exact reproductions to fulfill the inventory entries, completed the first phase of the recreation of this unique structure's three centuries of history.

As the restoration of Bacon's Castle has, since its inception, been perceived as a long-term project, the scope of this undertaking has both grown and changed. The most recent element in the endeavor is one that will

Aerial view of archaeological excavations on the site of the Bacon's Castle garden. The original size and layout of the 1680s garden are clearly visible.

have a tremendous impact upon the visitor to the site upon its completion—the restoration of a 1680s garden that is a full acre and a half in area, under the aegis of The Garden Club of Virginia. When the restoration of the garden was initially conceived, it was expected to encompass a rather straightforward interpretation of a nineteenth-century flower and vegetable garden, as recorded in a detailed drawing by the son of one of the dwelling's inhabitants in the Victorian era. In three years of archaeological excavations funded by The Garden Club, however, it became apparent that the nineteenth-century garden was only a mirror of the extremely rare and sophisticated seventeenth-century garden on which it was laid. Fragments of glass bell-jars, the foundations of a forcing wall, and indications of some type of garden structures revealed the highly developed nature of the horticulture practiced on the site. The restoration of the 1680s garden at Bacon's Castle will thus be another element in the APVA's interpretation of this uniquely significant Virginia site as it expanded and evolved over three centuries.

Mary Wingfield Scott, of Richmond, founded the APVA's William Byrd Branch in 1935, introducing innovative techniques to solve problems in urban preservation.

Innovations in Preservation

ven as the APVA contended with new standards in the restoration and interpretation of its museum properties, a further challenge in historic preservation asserted itself in the 1920s and '30s in the increasing threat to America's historic cityscapes from urban flux and the rigors of a depressed economy. Richmond's primary champion in the field of urban preservation was Mary Wingfield Scott, an accomplished architectural historian and a vocal advocate of the large-scale preservation of Richmond's historic neighborhoods on the model of Charleston, South Carolina. Moved to action in March 1935 by the imminent destruction of the Adam Craig House, a frame structure of about 1790 that was the childhood home of the heroine of Edgar Allan Poe's poem "To Helen," Mary Wingfield Scott formed the Craig House Committee, from which the APVA's William Byrd Branch evolved shortly thereafter.

From its earliest days, the William Byrd Branch's mission and methods of preserving Richmond's historic landmarks were recognized as being distinctly different from those of the APVA's other regional branches.

Faced with the formidable task of preserving numerous structures, city blocks, and even entire neighborhoods threatened by neglect, demolition, and new construction, without restricting the growth and dynamism of modern Richmond, Mary Wingfield Scott and the William Byrd Branch were forced to explore innovative methods of securing the preservation of threatened sites that did not require the outlay in funds, time, and effort of the full-scale historic house museum restoration. Thus, after the branch purchased and stabilized the Craig House in the mid-1930s, the property was leased to a variety of community-service organizations and housed an art center for blacks between 1938 and 1941, which was recognized as "a pioneering institution of its sort in the south" and later was merged with Virginia Union University. Through such successful adaptive reuse projects, Miss Scott believed that the branch could "extend indefinitely the work of the A.P.V.A., better than if we ourselves attempted to acquire and maintain a large numbers of museums or shrines."

The William Byrd Branch also pioneered the practice in Richmond of "revolving" historic properties by acquiring and

"Ten Thousand New Members Wanted," by Fred O. Seibel, <u>Richmond Times-Dispatch</u>, May 6, 1935.

restoring significant structures, then selling them subject to protective covenants and easements that secured specified historic elements from change or that safeguarded their historic context through the maintenance of a bulwark of surrounding land. The branch thus launched the effort to restore Richmond's historic Church Hill area in the 1950s with the purchase and restoration of two early-nineteenth-century structures, the Ann Carrington House and Hilary Baker House, both of which were later sold with restrictive covenants. The William Byrd Branch has continued through this method to play a major role in the preservation of Richmond's historic landmarks, including the Ellen Glasgow House (1841), the Wirt-Hancock-Caskie House (1805), and, most recently, the Pace-King House (1860) —an antebellum mansion in Richmond's Shockoe Bottom—which retains a remarkable portion of its original interior stenciling.

The parent organization of the APVA has also utilized several of the nontraditional

Top:
Preservation of the Adam
Craig House of 1790,
shown here in 1937 after
stabilization, was the immediate spur to the formation
of the William Byrd Branch.

Bottom:
The Pace-King House,
acquired by the APVA in
1975, was sold with protective covenants in 1987 to
safeguard its historic iron-
work and other significant
architectural features.

preservation techniques pioneered by the William Byrd Branch to maximize its effectiveness throughout Virginia. In two recent adaptive reuse ventures on the Eastern Shore, the APVA leased Holly Brook Plantation, a frame structure dating in its earliest parts to the late eighteenth century, as a bed-and-breakfast and the 1840s Hopkins & Brother Store in Onancock as a general store and ticket office. The sale of historic properties subject to easements has also been successfully employed, and, in 1984, the APVA initiated the "Virginia Fund," a revolving fund designed to enable the organization to acquire for resale or to locate a sympathetic purchaser for Virginia's properties facing destruction or decay. Through such techniques, the APVA has continued to be an effective force in Virginia preservation despite ever-changing conditions and needs.

Hopkins & Bro. Store, c. 1840, in Onancock, was acquired by the APVA in 1970 and is today leased for adaptive reuse as a general store and restaurant.

Interior view of Hopkins & Bro. Store.

*Opposite page, top:
An outstanding collection
of southern and English
furnishings of the eigh-
teenth century are featured
at Scotchtown.*

*Opposite page, bottom:
One of America's only historic bank museums, the
Farmers' Bank in
Petersburg of 1817 was
painstakingly restored by
the APVA and is main-
tained by the Fort Henry
Branch.*

*Bacon's Castle outbuild-
ings span Virginia's agri-
cultural history from the
early-eighteenth to mid-
twentieth centuries.*

*After extensive restoration
of the Marshall House in
the 1970s, research in the
early 1980s confirmed the
need for reinterpretation of
the southwest parlor. It now
serves, as it did for Marshall,
as a dining room.*

Katherine Stetson

Katherine Stetson

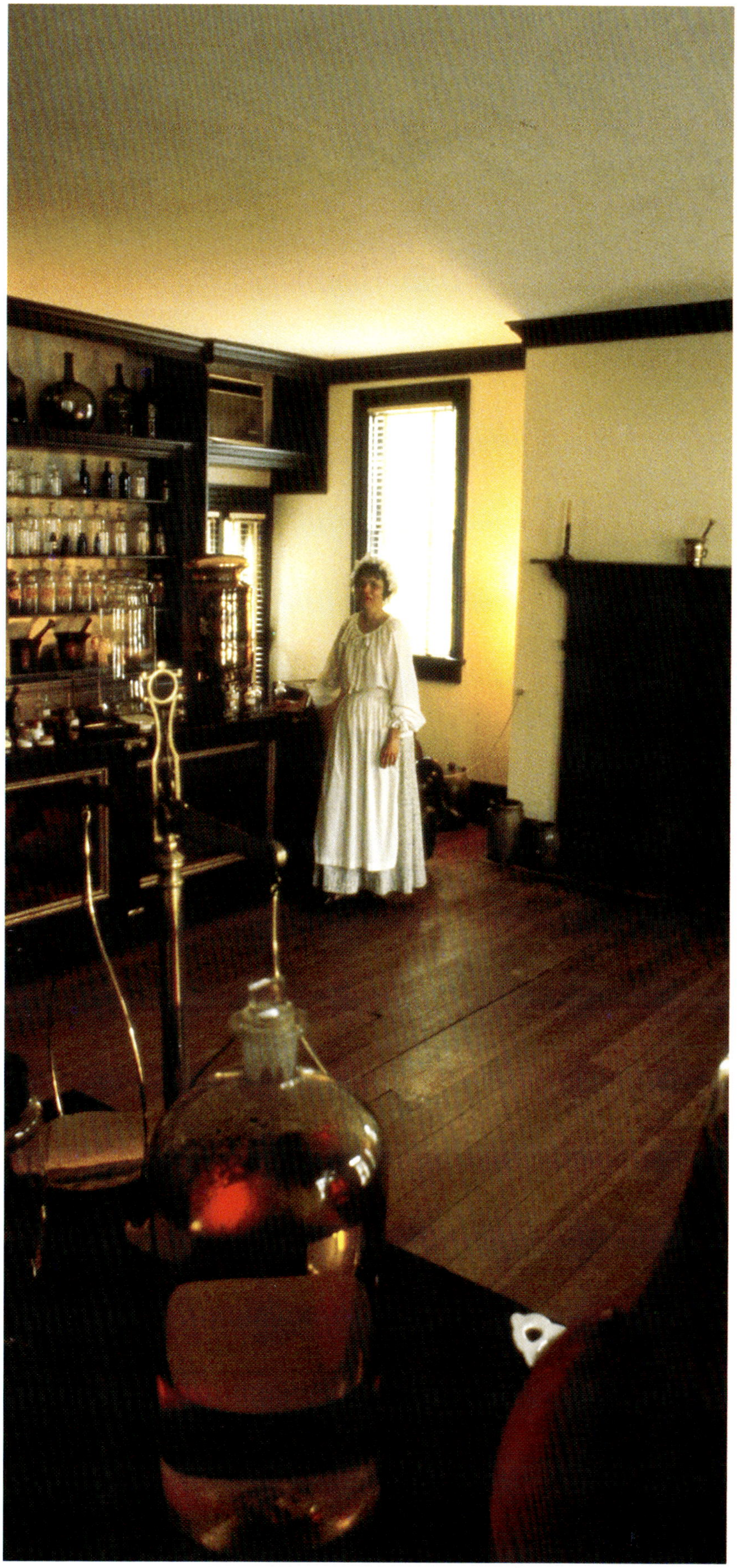

Katherine Wetzel

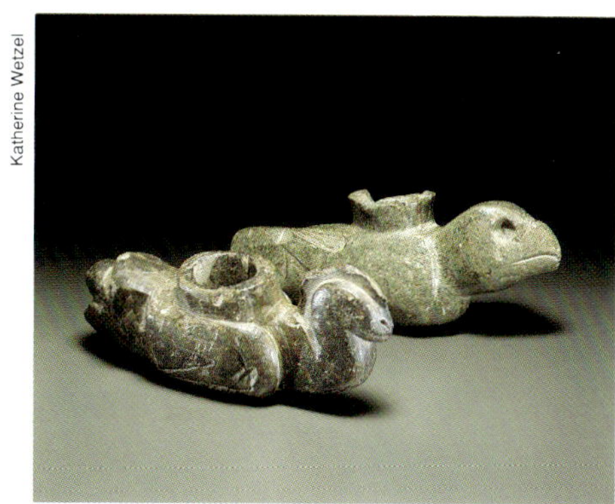

Ceremonial pipes of carved soapstone are among the oldest artifacts in the APVA's collections.

At the Hugh Mercer Apothecary Shop in Fredericksburg, acquired by the APVA in 1978, costumed interpreters explain eighteenth-century medicine surrounded by antique tools of the apothecary's trade.

*"Old Smithfield Church."
Bishop Meade, <u>Old
Churches, Ministers, and
Families of Virginia</u> (1857).
The restoration and main-
tenance of Saint Luke's
Church near Smithfield
were ongoing efforts of the
APVA's Isle of Wight
Branch for several decades.*

Preservation Outreach

*I*n addition to utilizing such preservation alternatives as adaptive reuse and revolving funds, the APVA has, since its inception, extended its preservationist influence throughout the commonwealth through its support for the preservation efforts of other organizations. Among the significant Virginia landmarks for whose restoration the APVA has contributed funding since 1889 are Gunston Hall, the University of Virginia, Kenmore, Stratford Hall, and Monticello.

In some cases, local APVA branches in the area of the endangered site have been inspired to make the preservation and restoration of that site their particular mission. In the earliest years of the association's existence, the Isle of Wight Branch took on the restoration of the seventeenth-century Saint Luke's Church near Smithfield—the structure on which the Jamestown Memorial Church was modeled in 1907. Though the Isle of Wight Branch contributed to and oversaw the restoration of Saint Luke's for many years, the property was never in the possession of the APVA. More recently, Prestwould, the monumental house built by Sir Peyton Skipwith in Mecklenburg County in 1795, was preserved as a local cultural center in 1963, due in large part to the efforts of the APVA's Roanoke River Branch and a substantial grant from the APVA parent organization.

Other branches of the APVA have devoted their efforts and energies toward the conservation of the more ephemeral elements of their community's history, particularly local archives. In addition to such activities as marking local historic sites, researching and indexing county records, and recording deteriorating tombstone inscriptions, several branches—notably those of Yorktown and Northampton—have made invaluable contributions to the preservation of Virginia history through their funding of county record-book restorations. In the same spirit, the APVA made several grants to the Virginia Colonial Records Project, in the 1950s and '60s, to microfilm British archives of particular significance to American history. Most recently, the APVA, under the direction of its late historian, Dr. Ransom B. True, undertook the Virginia Settlers Research Project—the compilation of a comprehensive biographical dictionary of more than twenty-five thousand Virginia settlers between 1607 and 1660.

Built by Sir Peyton Skipwith in 1795, Prestwould became a cultural center for Mecklenburg County due in large part to the efforts of the Roanoke River Branch of the APVA.

The Yorktown Branch of the APVA has been active since its earliest days in contributing to the restoration of York County record books, including <u>Judgements and Orders, 1763-1765</u>. In attendance at the volume's presentation were Mr. Charles Hatch, former historian of the National Park Service, Edith Elliott, court county clerk, and Mrs. Philip Donely, branch director.

In the last two decades, the APVA has also taken on the responsibility of sponsoring archaeological excavations on non-APVA sites threatened by development. Among such projects supported by the association was the excavation of the extensive Jordan's Point site which bore evidence of Indian inhabitation as early as 8000 B.C., long before its settlement by Samuel Jordan in 1619. Passing into the Bland family in the 1650s, the property was later the location of the beginning of Bacon's Rebellion in 1676. The APVA also supported exploratory archaeology at Blandfield, the Northern Neck plantation of the Beverley family in the eighteenth century, as part of the extensive restoration of the property being undertaken by its present owner.

Since its appeal for the preservation of Williamsburg's green spaces in the first decade of the twentieth century, the APVA has also lent its not inconsiderable voice to preservation issues of local, regional, and statewide significance. In 1951 the director of the William Byrd Branch noted of the APVA's campaign on behalf of Richmond preservation,

"We consider that some of our effective work has been in arousing public interest in the cause of preservation; for one has only to drive around Richmond to be conscious of the increasing number of individual property owners who have been influenced by our program of aspiration, solicitation, agitation and publication." The association thus registered vocal opposition to the demolition of several of Richmond's late-nineteenth-century downtown commercial buildings in 1971 and lobbied vigorously to achieve the passage of the city's historic zoning ordinance, based on the model of Charleston, and the preservation of Richmond's high-Victorian Gothic city hall.

In other facets of its role in educational outreach, the APVA has sponsored in its first century of preservation numerous lectures, seminars, and conferences. As early as 1895, a series of public lectures exploring various aspects of Virginia history was delivered in the hall of Virginia's House of Delegates by such renowned historians as Lyon G. Tyler and Philip Bruce, the latter a member of the association's all-male advisory board of the period. More recently, in 1976, the APVA initiated the Jamestown Archaeology Conference, to provide a professional forum for current issues in Virginia archaeology. The APVA has also shared its growing expertise in the technology of historic preservation, derived in large part from the ongoing maintenance and restoration of the thirty-five historic properties under its care. In the mid-1970s, the association offered consulting services by its professional restoration staff for the analysis of historic paint colors and masonry restoration, while a seminar in techniques of masonry conservation, entitled "Keeping It Together," was held in 1984 and 1985 for those interested in practicing hands-on restoration. Through such services and outreach activities, the APVA continues to broaden its scope and its achievements in the preservation of Virginia's past, while it reaches and inspires an ever-larger audience.

The APVA's 1986 acquisition of Pear Valley—a rare vernacular survivor of the colonial era on Virginia's Eastern Shore—represents recent shifts in concepts of architectural and historical worth.

The Second Century

The APVA of 1989 is a different creature from the organization created by Mary Jeffery Galt and Cynthia Beverley Tucker Coleman in 1889, as it reflects the myriad changes that have occurred in one of the most volatile centuries in man's history. The historic preservation field itself, essentially nonexistent in 1889, has emerged and matured over these hundred years into a discipline with increasingly specialized requirements and training programs. Attitudes toward preservation have also altered drastically in the last century, and the criteria for the evaluation of a threatened site's merit have become ever broader and more objective. Technology, in particular, has advanced in ways undreamed of in 1889, presenting both new hazards and new solutions for historic sites. Above all American society has experienced revolutionary change, and the attribution of specific moral and social values to historic monuments and characters becomes increasingly imperceptible in our preservation and presentation of the past. Nor are the goals of preservation any longer the select purview of women, as guardians of the public morality, or of the socially elite.

At the same time, today's APVA is very much a product of those earlier goals, motivations, and personalities. A tribute to Mary Jeffery Galt written after her death in 1922 elaborated on the debt that the APVA owed its founders in terms that are equally accurate today: "To such women the A.P.V.A. owes its origins and its achievements, they worked to preserve the memorials of the past, and in so doing they handed down a priceless legacy to the future."

The APVA of 1989 is thus the product of each individual who left his or her impression upon the organization and each year through which it struggled or thrived. The properties it maintains, the collections it preserves, the activities it carries out, and the influence that it has exerted on behalf of preservation elsewhere in Virginia and in America are an amalgam of the motives of past and present. The result is an organization that can truly claim to have preserved a microcosm of well over three centuries of Virginia's history. With properties that range in date from Virginia and America's earliest origins to the present, in function from bank to debtors'

The APVA's contributions to the preservation of Virginia's economic and industrial history range from the restoration and maintenance (by the Ralph Wormeley Branch) of an eighteenth-century tobacco warehouse in Urbanna (top) to the sponsorship (by the William Byrd Branch) of archaeological excavations on the site of an urban ironworks and armory—the Virginia Manufactory of Arms, in Richmond (bottom).

prison and church to courthouse, and in degree from yeoman's cottage to manor house, the APVA has a truly remarkable record in the preservation of one region's history. If one adds to this record those sites and objects in whose discovery and preservation the APVA has played a role, the history thus preserved spans the millenia.

As the APVA embarks upon its second century of preservation in Virginia, it can reflect upon one hundred years of inspiration, struggles, and successes, and can look forward to another hundred years of the same, having proved itself to be a vital and viable preservation force in the face of adversity and change. A vision of the APVA recorded in 1928 is one reflecting the single goal that has guided the association's first century of battling destruction and decay and that will lead it into the next century: "Such work as this Association does is never finished; as we advance, the horizon of our work advances, and we see beyond still more important work to be done."

The spiritual life of several centuries has been preserved through one hundred years of APVA efforts, including the restoration of such monuments as the Page family tombs in the Abingdon Church graveyard in Gloucester (top), and the maintenance of the Memorial Church of 1907 at Jamestown (bottom), which continues to be the site of modern wedding celebrations.

The legal and governmental history of Virginia is well represented in the APVA's collection of structures, such as the Isle of Wight County courthouse, in Smithfield, and objects, including an eighteenth-century raised-panel bookcase that still stands in the Northampton County courthouse for which it was originally constructed.

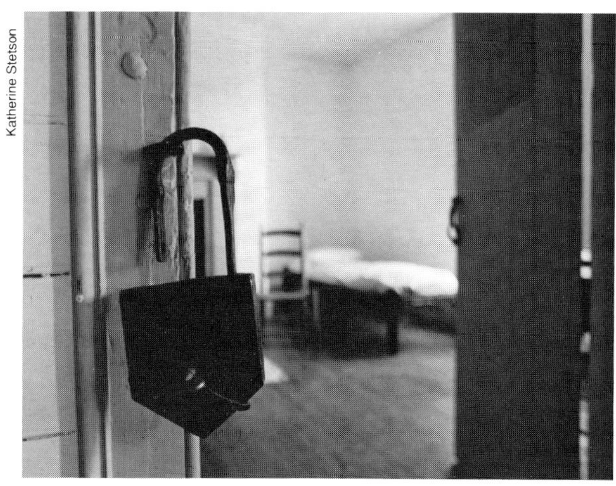

The APVA has been instrumental in preserving a cross-section of centuries of commerce and credit in Virginia, including the Debtors' Prison of 1782 in Accomac, restored by the Drummondtown Branch (top), the Debtors' Prison of 1814 in Eastville, maintained by the Northampton Branch (center), and Hopkins Store of the 1840s, which retains original store fittings, including a Victorian cash register still in regular use (bottom).

Opposite page:
In 1986, the APVA took on a new role in Williamsburg through the lease of the Dora Armistead House. Owned by just one family since its construction in 1890 and retaining a remarkable collection of original family possessions, the Armistead House is a unique survivor of pre-restoration Williamsburg.

From forts to homes, the APVA collections span centuries of struggle and survival in Virginia.
(Top): Military artifacts found over the past century at Jamestown range from Indian arrowheads and early colonial swordhilts to bullets of Civil War vintage.

(Bottom):Excavations at Smith's Fort Plantation revealed remains of the defensive earthworks erected by John Smith in 1608.
(Center): For a short time, Bacon's Castle, depicted here in an elevation drawing by Stephen A. Smith, was a rebel stronghold in Bacon's Rebellion of 1676.

Properties Owned, Leased or Maintained by the APVA 1889-1989

Name	Location	Date	Acquired	Transferred
Jamestown	James City Co.	1607	1892	
Second Site of St. John's Church	Hampton	1623	1912	1986
Warner Hall Graveyard	Gloucester Co.	1662	1903	
Bacon's Castle	Surry Co.	1665	1973	
Custis Tombs	Northampton Co.	1696	1968	
Pear Valley	Northampton Co.	18th century	1986	
Eagle's Nest	Charles City	18th century	1979	1981
Powhatan's Chimney	Gloucester Co.	18th century		1978
Capitol Site	Williamsburg	1704	1897	1928
Jail	Williamsburg	1702	1929	1933
Powder Magazine	Williamsburg	1715	1890	1986
Scotchtown	Hanover Co.	1719	1958	
Lynnhaven House	Virginia Beach	1724	1971	
Site of Secretary Nelson's House	Yorktown	1725	1928	
Old Clerk's Office	Eastville	1731	1913	
Old Courthouse	Eastville	1731	1913	
Smith's Fort Plantation	Surry Co.	1735	1933	
Cub Creek Church Site	Charlotte Co.	1738	1938	
Isle of Wight Courthouse	Smithfield	1750	1938	
Saint Paul's Church Site	Suffolk	1753	1929	
Tobacco Warehouse	Urbanna	1760	1938	
Rising Sun Tavern	Fredericksburg	1760	1907	
Hugh Mercer Apothecary Shop	Fredericksburg	1770	1978	
Saint James's Cottage	Fredericksburg	1770	1974	
Smithfield Plantation	Montgomery Co.	1772	1961	
Mary Washington House	Fredericksburg	1772	1890	
Old Stone House	Richmond	1775	1912	
Holly Brook Plantation	Northampton Co.	1775	1982	
Lord Dunmore's Ice House	Williamsburg	1775	1900	1933
Debtors' Prison	Accomac	1782	1910	
Adam Craig House	Richmond	1785	1935	1986
Debtors' Prison	Prince Edward Co.	1787	1951	1975
Monmouth Church Site	Rockbridge Co.	1788	1897	1975

Name	Location	Date	Acquired	Transferred
John Marshall House	Richmond	1790	1911	
Roaring Springs	Gloucester Co.	1790	1978	
Cape Henry Lighthouse	Virginia Beach	1791	1930	
Elm Hill	Mecklenburg Co.	1800	1982	1987
Wirt-Hancock-Caskie House	Richmond	1805	1970	1981
Ann Carrington House	Richmond	1810	1944	1973
Hilary Baker House	Richmond	1810	1959	1973
Thomas Reed's Clerk's Office	Charlotte Co	1810	rebuilt	
Nathaniel Friend House	Petersburg	1810	1968	1976
Debtors' Prison	Eastville	1814	1913	
McIlwaine House	Petersburg	1816	1973	1981
Gay Mont	Caroline Co.	1816	1976	
Farmers' Bank	Petersburg	1817	1966	
Ball Cemetery	Loudoun Co.	1837	1895	
Maple Roads	Charlotte Co.	1830	1984	1988
Hopkins & Bros. Store and Steamship Office	Onancock	1840	1970	
Hardgrove House	Richmond	1840	1985	
202, 204, 206 & 208 North 19th Street	Richmond	1840s & 1890s	1980	1986
Ellen Glasgow House	Richmond	1841	1947	1983
Elmira Shelton House	Richmond	1844	1957	1957
Walter Reed Birthplace	Gloucester	1850	1968	
Pace-King House	Richmond	1850	1975	1987
Pulliam House	Richmond	1856	1938	1966
Cosby Mill & Miller's House	Augusta Co.	1890	1980	1984
Dora Armistead House	Williamsburg	1890	1985	
Gabriella Page House	Richmond	1930	1948	1985

APVA Presidents 1889-1989

Mrs. Fitzhugh Lee
(Ellen Bernard)
1889-1890

Mrs. Joseph Bryan
(Isobel Lamont Stewart)
1890-1910

Mrs. J. Taylor Ellyson
(Lora Hotchkiss)
1910-1935

Mrs. Arthur P. Wilmer
(Margaret W.)
1935-1945

Miss Gabriella Page
1945-1949

Mrs. Douglas Southall Freeman
(Inez Goddin)
1949-1953

Mrs. Brockenbrough Lamb
(Janie Preston Boulware)
1953-1964

Mrs. W. Taliaferro Thompson
(Jessie Gresham Baker)
1964-1968

Mrs. Robert I. Boswell
(Bruce Looney)
1968-1969

Mrs. John W. Riely
(Jean Roy Jones)
1969-1972

Mr. Elbert Cox
1972-1974

Mrs. Kenneth R. Higgins
(Mary Douthat Smith)
1974-1976

Mr. James W. Rawles
1976-1979

Mr. Robert H. Garbee
1979-1982

Mrs. Robert Woodrow Cabaniss
(Florence Smelley)
1982-1984

Mrs. John H. Van Landingham, III
(Shirley Turner)
1984-1986

Mrs. Benjamin W. Mears, Jr.,
(Katherine Turner)

APVA Branches 1989